From the library of

The Golden Book of Stars and Planets

By Judith Herbst
Illustrated by Tom LaPadula

Photographs courtesy of NASA

Consultant: Mark R. Chartrand, Ph.D., Vice President of the National Space Society

For Carol Backman, my great friend
—J.H.

A GOLDEN BOOK • NEW YORK
Western Publishing Company, Inc., Racine, Wisconsin 53404

THE FIRST ASTRONOMERS

Long, long ago there were the stars. They shined for all the creatures on Earth. They shined for the fish, and the birds, and the fierce tigers. But the animals didn't stop to look at the stars. Only the people looked, and they were filled with wonder at what they saw.

The nights long ago were dark and deep. There were no bright cities. There was no pollution to block out the light of the stars. So the first people on Earth had the very best view of the sky. They could see many more stars than we can see. The twinkling night sky must have seemed like a magical place.

The first people sat around their crackling fires and wondered what the stars were. They watched the stars move slowly across the sky each night. Soon the people were imagining that the stars formed pictures. They saw bears, and tigers, and brave hunters up in the sky. So they started to make up stories about the star pictures.

The people also saw the moon change its shape little by little every night. "What's happening?" they asked, but no one knew. Then a few people began to draw the moon's shapes on the walls of their caves. The cave people were watching and learning. They were the first astronomers.

6

Years passed, and the people learned to be farmers. As the months went by, the farmers began to see different groups of stars in the sky. Some stars told the farmers it was time to plant. Other stars meant it was time to gather in the crops. Still other stars warned the farmers that winter was coming. The farmers learned to be star watchers, too.

Then one day the people looked out across the wide green ocean. They had seen the ocean many times before. But on this day the people had a wonderful idea. They decided to build something that would carry them over the ocean. The people became sailors.

One of the first things the sailors learned was how the stars moved. Stars rise in the east, just like the sun. They travel slowly across the sky and set in the west. So the sailors looked for a very bright star. A little while later they looked for the star again, but the star was in a different place. It had moved. If the star was rising in the sky, the sailors knew they were facing east. If the star was setting, they knew they were facing west. The stars kept the sailors on a straight course.

But it was the ancient Greeks who discovered that a few of the stars did not move together with all the others. Some traveled slower. Others traveled faster. Some even seemed to be traveling backward! The Greeks called these strange stars planets, which means "wanderers."

The Greeks could see Mercury, Venus, Mars, Jupiter, and Saturn. You can see the same five planets, too, and sometimes you can even see the planet Uranus. But you must know just where to look.

The first star watchers did not have telescopes. They did not have cameras or special tools to teach them about the sky. But they did have their eyes, and that is the best tool of all.

The people looked up into the twinkling midnight sky. They saw the great beauty of the stars. Something stirred inside the people. They wanted to build a special place just to watch the stars. They wanted to build a grand tower with windows that opened to the night. They wanted to build an observatory.

In Mexico you can see the observatory that the ancient Indians built long ago. It is called El Caracol. El Caracol means "The Snail" in Spanish. El Caracol is crumbling now. The jungle plants are slowly covering its stone walls. But El Caracol is still very beautiful.

Night after night the Mexican astronomers watched Venus from the window of El Caracol. They learned when Venus would rise and set. They learned just where it would be on every day of the year. El Caracol was a wonderful observatory, even without a telescope.

The years rolled on. Astronomers came and went. Each one discovered a little more about the sky. But studying the stars and planets was awfully hard. Everything except the moon looked like a tiny silver dot. If only the astronomers could see better!

But then, in 1564, a great astronomer was born in Italy. His name was Galileo. Galileo did not start out to be an astronomer. At first he was more interested in mathematics. But one day word of a fabulous invention reached him. It was a long tube with lenses inside. The lenses had to be set in just the right way, and then the tube would make faraway things look bigger and closer. The new invention was called a telescope.

Galileo became very excited. He knew the telescope would be a great tool for astronomers. So Galileo got busy, and in a few months he had built a telescope of his very own. Galileo's telescope wasn't as powerful as a modern telescope, but it worked.

Galileo quickly aimed his telescope at the moon. Wow! The moon had mountains! Then he aimed his telescope at Saturn. He could hardly believe his eyes. Saturn had rings! Then one night Galileo pointed his telescope at Jupiter. He saw a big dot, which was Jupiter, and four tiny dots—Jupiter's moons. Nobody had ever seen Jupiter's moons before. These four moons are called the Galilean satellites, in honor of Galileo.

The telescope was like a magical key. It opened up the universe for astronomers. The dark night sky would never look the same again.

Uranus

Asteroids

Saturn

Mercury

Earth

Sun

Venus

Mars

Planets move two different ways in space. They travel around the sun in great oval paths. These paths are called orbits. The farther away from the sun a planet is, the slower its orbit. Planets also turn round and round like spinning toy tops. The time it takes a planet to turn around once is called its day. The time it takes a planet to go around the sun once is called a year.

A SOLAR SYSTEM IS BORN

Earth is part of a special family. We call this family our solar system. There is nothing exactly like it in the whole universe. Our solar system has little planets made of rock. It has giant planets made of gas. There are even striped planets! There are frozen moons and tiny worlds no bigger than a baseball. But our solar system did not always look like this.

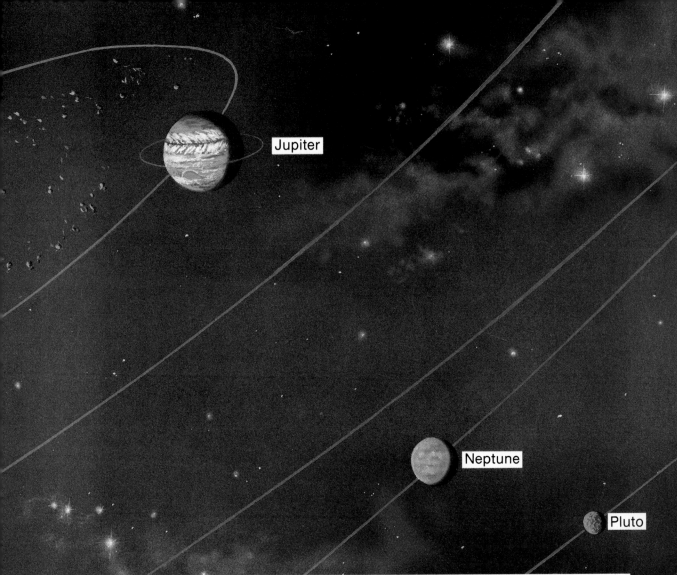

Jupiter

Neptune

Pluto

Once upon a long, long time there was a great cloud in space. The cloud was made of gas and tiny bits of dust. It turned very slowly like a wheel.

Nothing much happened for a great while. Millions of years passed. The cloud kept on turning very slowly. But little by little the cloud was picking up speed. It began to spin a little faster. It began to spin much faster. All the bits and pieces of dust began sticking together. The cloud was getting lumpy.

What do you think happened to the cloud?

The lumps became clumps.

The clumps became chunks.

The chunks became rocks.

And the rocks became…the nine planets and their moons!

Meanwhile, strange things were happening to the gas in the center of the cloud. It was beginning to twist and swirl. Slowly the gas began to shape itself into a huge ball. The ball of gas grew so hot, it started to glow. Then it started to shine. The mighty ball of gas became the sun. A solar system was born in space.

The Sun

The sun is the real big shot in our solar system because everything travels around it. Earth takes 365¼ days to make the trip. We call that one year. Mars is not as close to the sun as we are, so Mars needs almost two Earth years to go all the way around. But poor little Pluto has the longest journey of all. It takes Pluto 247 Earth years to go once around the sun.

The sun is just another star. It is not the biggest star. It is not the hottest or the brightest star. But the sun is very special to us. It lights up our planet and keeps us warm. It helps plants and animals grow. Without the sun, there would be no life on Earth.

The sun is 93 million miles away from us. If you could travel to the sun in a car, it would take you 176 years to get there. But the sun is really the closest star to Earth. The next closest star is trillions of miles farther away than the sun.

The sun and Earth's moon are always moving across the sky, but they do not move along together.

They take different paths and move at different speeds. But once in a long while the moon catches up to the sun.

Sometimes it crosses right in front of the sun. Then for a few minutes we can't see the sun because the moon is in the way. We see a total eclipse of the sun. During the eclipse the moon looks like it is wearing a flaming crown. But it is really just the edges of the sun peeking out. Scientists call this the sun's corona. Corona means "crown" in Latin.

The corona doesn't give off much light, so the sky grows dark during the eclipse. Many animals are fooled. They think it is night. Some of them even go to sleep. The flowers are fooled, too. They close their petals.

The moon keeps moving, so the eclipse only lasts a few minutes. You should never look directly at an eclipse. It can damage your eyes.

Even though the sun is so close, it is hard to study. The sun is a giant ball of very hot gas. It is brighter than 400,000,000,000,000,000,000,000,000 (400 septillion) light bulbs. So astronomers have to use a special kind of telescope to look at the sun. If they are not careful, they could burn their eyes. No one should *ever* look directly at the sun.

The sun is not a very quiet place at all. It is like a stormy ocean. Giant waves of gas shoot far out into space. Some of the waves are thousands of miles high. That is bigger than anything on Earth. That is even bigger than Earth itself.

THE SUPER-TERRIFIC PLANET TRIP

Mercury, The Fire Planet

Mercury is 36 million miles from the sun. It is not a very good place for a vacation. It is hot enough on Mercury to bake pizza.

Mercury is a speedy little planet. It zooms around the sun in just 88 days. That is Mercury's year. But a day on Mercury is very, very long. It lasts for 1,407 hours!

Mercury would certainly be a strange place to live. Mercury has no clouds and no weather. It has no air, and there is nothing to make Mercury's sky blue. If you could stand on Mercury, the sun would look like a gigantic bright star in a jet-black sky.

Mercury is dusty and gray. There are no rivers or oceans. It is just a big ball of rock. There are deep holes called craters everywhere. The craters are many miles wide. Mercury also has mountains and volcanoes, but the volcanoes don't erupt anymore. Nothing moves on Mercury. It is a still, silent world.

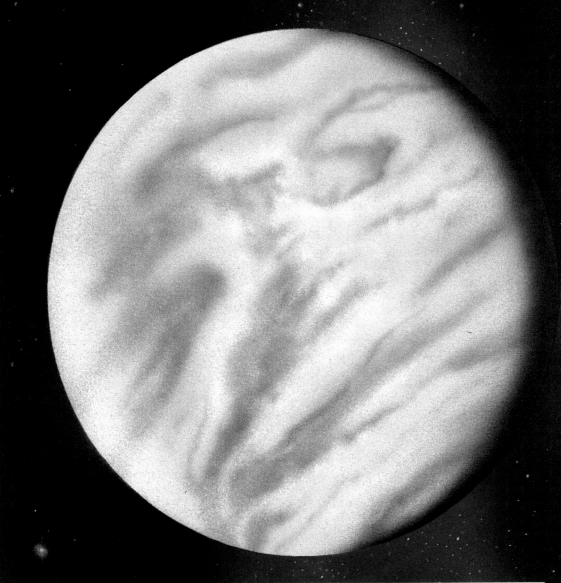

Venus, The Mystery Planet

Venus is the mystery planet. It is covered by thick clouds. The clouds hide Venus' surface, so for a long time nobody knew what Venus looked like. Some people thought Venus was a jungle. They thought there were strange plants and animals on Venus. Were they wrong!

Venus is farther from the sun than Mercury, but it is hotter. That's because the clouds keep Venus warm like a heavy blanket. There is water on Venus, but it is not on the surface. There are no great lakes or oceans. It is so hot on Venus that all the surface water boiled away. It turned to steam and rose high into the clouds. Then the water mixed with poison gases in the clouds. It turned into a very strong acid. Sometimes a light rain of acid falls on Venus.

Scientists are not too sure what it is like on Venus. But they know that Venus has a huge mountain chain. The mountains are named Maxwell Montes. Montes means "mountains" in Italian. Maxwell Montes are over seven miles high. The tallest mountains on Earth are only five miles high. Maxwell Montes might be the tallest mountain chain in the whole solar system.

15

Earth, The Perfect Planet

Earth is the third planet from the sun. It is the only planet with great oceans of water. That's because Earth is in the perfect spot. If Earth were closer to the sun, the oceans would boil away. If Earth were farther from the sun, the oceans would freeze to ice. Then there could be no life.

Life began in the oceans, but billions of years ago there was no life anywhere at all on Earth. There weren't even any oceans. Earth had just been born. It was a brand-new planet. The land shook and cracked as Earth started to cool off. Meteors crash-landed everywhere. Then it began to rain. It rained for thousands and thousands of years. Soon the deepest parts of the land had filled with water. They became the oceans.

The early oceans were like thin soup. The soup was mostly water with some poison gases mixed in. Nothing much happened to the soup for a long time, but slowly the sun began to warm the ocean water. The soup began to cook. Flashes of lightning zapped the soup with energy. The soup got thicker.

Something amazing was happening to the oceans. Little by little life was beginning to form deep within the waters. That is why scientists call water the liquid of life.

Earth is wrapped in a thick blanket of gases. These gases are Earth's atmosphere. The part of the atmosphere that is closest to the ground is the air we breathe. But Earth's atmosphere stretches up and up and up for many hundreds of miles into space. Astronomers can use special cameras to see Earth's atmosphere from space. It is a very beautiful sight. It covers our planet like a golden flame.

Earth's atmosphere is very important to life. It protects us from the dangerous rays that stream out from the sun. Some of these rays are the kind that can give us a bad sunburn when we go to the beach. So if Earth did not have an atmosphere, all of these dangerous rays would get through.

Earth has six giant chunks of land that stick up through the water. These chunks of land are called continents. There is also a fabulous ice continent at Earth's South Pole, making it seven continents in all. No other planet in the solar system has continents. And no other planet in the solar system has life.

Earth is special indeed.

The moon is Earth's satellite. It travels around Earth like a race car zooming around a track. The moon moves pretty fast. It flies along at over 2,300 miles an hour, but it still takes the moon 28 days to go once around Earth.

Earth's Moon

Earth is not alone on its journey around the sun. It has a partner in space—a rocky little world we call the moon. Earth and the moon are strange space partners. They are as different as two places can be. Earth is filled with color and life, while the moon is dusty and gray. Nothing lives on the moon. Nothing even moves. The moon looks bright and friendly shining in the nighttime sky. But it is one of the loneliest places in the solar system.

Walking on the moon would be very spooky. The moon has no air, so you would have to wear a full space suit and a helmet. The moon has no water and no weather, so the sky above is always jet black. You would be able to see many more stars than you can see from Earth. The sky above would blaze with silver starlight.

You would have to be very careful as you walked across the surface of the moon. You would not weigh as much as you do on Earth. If you weigh 100 pounds on Earth, you would only weigh 16 pounds on the moon. So you would bounce and float like a giant beach ball. That sounds like fun, but it could be dangerous. It would be easy to trip on a moon rock and fall.

There are craters almost everywhere you look on the moon. Some craters are very small, like potholes, and some craters are really huge. Clavius Crater is big enough to swallow up Connecticut, Rhode Island, and Massachusetts. If you could drive around Clavius Crater in a car, it would take you almost nine hours.

The moon also has tall mountain chains that go on and on for many miles, but the mountains are bare. There are no trees or bushes growing along the slopes. There are no mountain streams. There are only loose rocks and a thin layer of gray dust on the ground.

Scientists think the moon is the same age as Earth, but they are not sure where the moon came from. Maybe it formed from the great solar system birth cloud. Or perhaps the moon was once part of Earth, and then, billions of years ago, it somehow broke away.

The moon may be our closest neighbor in space, but it is still a strange and mysterious world.

In 1969 three astronauts traveled to the moon in a spacecraft called *Apollo 11*. It took them three days to get there. The trip was very special. It was the first time people had ever gone to another world. The astronauts were explorers. They walked around and gathered rocks to bring home. They left a lot of footprints. The footprints will be there forever. The moon has no wind to blow them away.

Mars, The Red Planet

Mars is called the Red Planet. It's easy to see why. All the other planets shine silver in the dark night sky. But Mars looks like a little copper dot.

Mars is covered by a layer of soft red sand. Sometimes mighty dust storms blow across Mars and send the sand swirling and flying. The Martian sky fills up with orange dust. If you were caught in a Martian sandstorm, you would not be able to see anything. You would not be able to walk or even stand up. The Martian winds are very strong. They are like tornadoes on Earth.

But there are nice days on Mars, too. The fierce winds become gentle breezes, the dust settles, and the sun comes out. The temperature can go all the way up to minus 9 degrees Fahrenheit. That is about as cold as it gets in Minnesota in winter.

If you wore a special space suit, you could walk around on Mars. You would have to bring your own air, though. The air on Mars is very, very thin, so there is almost nothing to breathe. You would have to bring your own water, too. Mars has a little bit of water, but it is all frozen. In the winter you would see some frost on the ground, but you would never see snow.

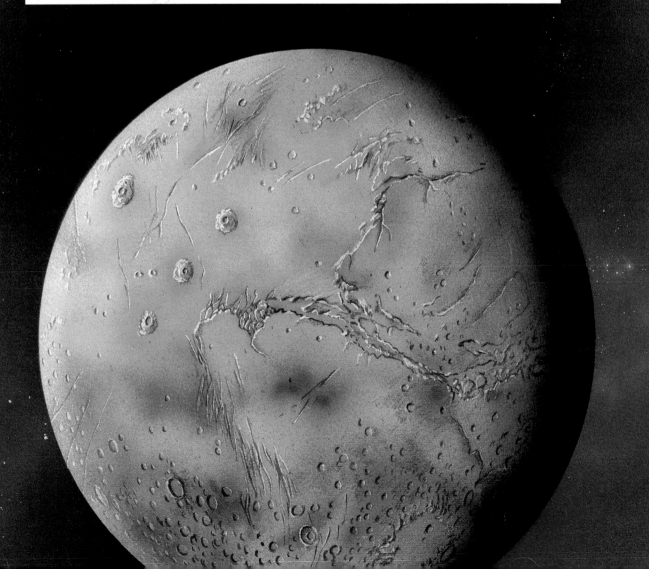

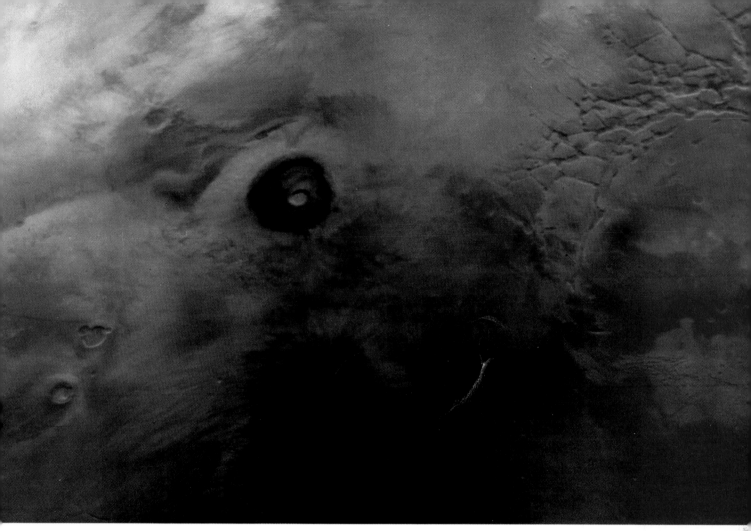

Olympus Mons

Mars has the largest volcano in the solar system. It is called Olympus Mons. Olympus Mons is a real giant. It is over 16 miles high. The biggest volcano on Earth is only five miles high.

Mars also has mighty canyons. The canyons run across the planet for many miles. They look like tremendous cracks in the Martian surface. One canyon is over four miles deep. That is deep enough to hold 16 Empire State Buildings one on top of the other.

If you could walk far enough on Mars, you would come to the famous Martian sand dunes. The sand dunes are huge mounds of peach-colored sand. The dunes sway and flow when the great Martian winds blow.

But the biggest mystery of all is the Martian channels. The channels are great deep grooves. They twist and bend like long, lazy rivers, but the rivers are as dry as dust. They have no water. So the scientists are very puzzled. If there is no flowing water on Mars, what made the channels? Did Mars once have rushing rivers? Did Mars once have life?

Flying Rocks—The Asteroids

If you journey past Mars, you will come to the asteroids. The word *asteroid* means "little star," but the asteroids are not stars. They are chunks of rock that circle the sun mostly between Mars and Jupiter. Each asteroid travels along its own path, but some move close together in a pack, so the asteroids are like a swarm of bees buzzing around a hive. The biggest asteroid is named Ceres, but being the biggest doesn't mean much. Ceres is so small, you could drive across it in about two days.

There are thousands and thousands of asteroids. Scientists don't know exactly how many there are. Most of the asteroids are too small to see through a telescope, but scientists have been able to study some of the bigger ones. They know that the asteroids have funny shapes. They are not round like planets. They have rough edges and craters. A lot of asteroids look like potatoes, so that started some scientists wondering.

"Hmm," they said. "The asteroids look like something that broke apart."

But other scientists said, "Maybe the asteroids are pieces that were left over when the planets formed long, long ago."

These are good guesses. But, so far, no one has solved the riddle of the asteroids.

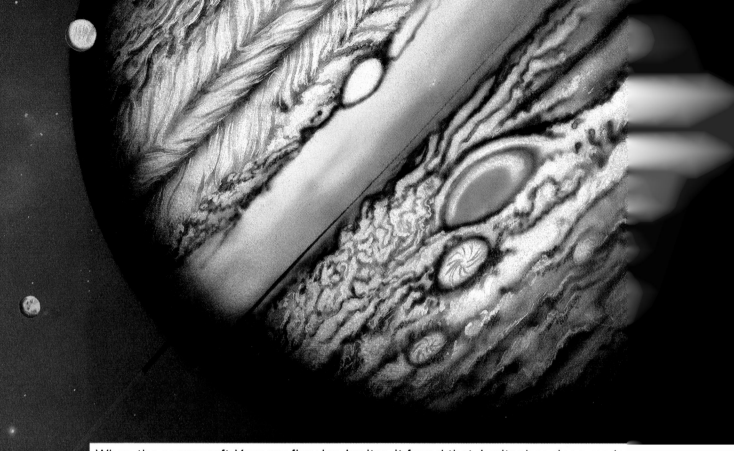

When the spacecraft *Voyager* flew by Jupiter, it found that Jupiter has rings made of tiny bits of dirt and ice. The Great Red Spot is in the center below the rings.

Jupiter, The Gas Planet

Jupiter is the biggest planet in the solar system. It is not made of rock like the first four planets. Jupiter is a giant ball of gas. A spaceship could never land on Jupiter. It would just sink down and down and down through the gas.

Jupiter is covered by a thick layer of clouds. The clouds are red, yellow, white, and orange. They make Jupiter look like a striped beach ball.

Jupiter's clouds shift and flow. They are never still. Scientists use great telescopes with special cameras to watch the clouds move. Furious winds send the clouds round and round Jupiter. The winds that blow across some parts of Jupiter can reach 250 miles an hour. That is faster than a speeding train.

Jupiter is famous for its Great Red Spot. Scientists think the Red Spot is a huge storm in the top layers of the clouds. The Red Spot is so big, six Earths could fit inside it.

Jupiter is such a weird planet, you would probably think that life could never start there. But scientists are not so sure. Jupiter's clouds are a lot like the soup of life on early Earth. Who knows? Maybe very simple life is forming high in Jupiter's cloud tops right now.

The Monster's Moons

No one is really sure how many moons Jupiter has. At first scientists thought Jupiter had 12 moons. Then they counted 14. But the more scientists study the *Voyager* photos, the more moons they find.

Here are the four moons Galileo saw through his little telescope so many years ago. To Galileo, they looked like tiny silver dots. Would he have been surprised!

Io looks like a pizza hot out of the oven. That's because Io is covered with volcanoes. The volcanoes erupt again and again. Burning sulfur spills over their sides.

Scientists call Ganymede the Ice Giant. Ganymede is Jupiter's biggest moon. It is bigger than the planet Mercury! Scientists think Ganymede has a very thick layer of ice just below its surface.

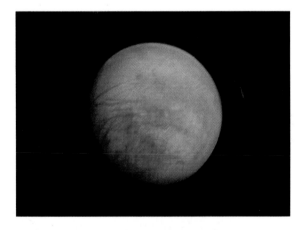

Europa may have the strangest volcanoes in the whole solar system. Some scientists think Europa's volcanoes erupt snowflakes and frozen water. Europa also appears to have hundreds of crisscrossing lines.

Callisto is over a million miles from Jupiter. It is covered with craters, but there is ice just below the dark surface. In the middle of Jupiter's summer the temperature on Callisto only gets as high as 190 degrees below zero.

Saturn, The Great Ringed Planet

Nobody knew Saturn had rings until 1656, when the astronomer Christian Huygens saw them through his telescope. Then, in 1980, the spacecraft *Voyager 1* flew past Saturn and took the first close-up pictures of the rings. The *Voyager* pictures show that Saturn's beautiful rings are really tiny chunks of rock and ice. The ring chunks circle Saturn like millions of little moons. Several small real moons keep the chunks on course. The moons act like shepherds tending their flock. If a ring chunk tries to get away and escape into space, one of the moons pushes it back in place.

Saturn is a huge gas planet, just like Jupiter. But the winds on Saturn blow much harder and faster than the winds on Jupiter. The winds at Saturn's equator can reach 1,000 miles an hour!

One of the strangest things about Saturn is its weight. Saturn is the second largest planet in the solar system, but it is very light. If you could put Saturn into a giant swimming pool, it would float!

Saturn has the biggest moon in the solar system. It is named Titan. Scientists think Titan is covered by gooey tar. They think Titan may look like Earth did billions of years ago, but there is so much smog on Titan, *Voyager* could not get any good pictures.

Titan

Uranus has 11 thin rings. The rings are made out of tiny bits of ice and dust. But Uranus is so tilted, the rings circle the planet in a strange way. They make Uranus look as if it were jumping through a hoop.

Uranus, Just Rolling Along

Uranus is a dark, frozen world. Ever so slowly, it makes its way around the sun. It takes Uranus 84 Earth years to circle the sun just once. That's because Uranus is so far away.

Uranus is strange indeed. All the other planets turn round and round like twirling ballerinas, but not Uranus. Uranus is tilted. It is tilted so much, it is like a ballerina who fell over. So instead of spinning right-side up, Uranus is rolling on its side!

What happened? A few scientists think that Uranus had an accident millions of years ago. They think something very large crashed into Uranus and knocked it over. Maybe it was a giant asteroid or a runaway moon. But whatever hit Uranus had to be at least as big as Earth.

The top layer of Uranus is frozen gas. Beneath the gas there is a thick layer of water and poison liquid. One of the poison liquids is ammonia. It is a lot like the ammonia that people use to clean their homes. The very center of Uranus is metal.

Once scientists thought Uranus had five moons, but when *Voyager* flew past Uranus, it found ten more! The new moons are close to Uranus' ring band, and they are much, much smaller than the main moons.

The Lost Worlds of Neptune and Pluto

Neptune and Pluto are the last two planets in the solar system. They are so far away that scientists can hardly see them. Even through giant telescopes, Neptune and Pluto look like little fuzzy blobs. But scientists have discovered a few things about these two lost worlds.

They know that Neptune is a lot like its neighbor Uranus. Neptune is almost exactly the same size as Uranus. Both are made of gas with metal in the middle, but Neptune likes to hide from the scientists under a thin layer of fog. Sometimes the fog covers half the planet for many days. Then, suddenly, it clears. Scientists don't know what the fog is made of or how it forms.

Pluto is a real puzzle. It is not at all like Neptune. It is not like Jupiter, or Saturn, or Uranus. Pluto is not even made of gas! Pluto is made of rock like the first four planets. Scientists think that is very weird. What is Pluto doing all the way out there with the gas planets?

Many scientists think that Pluto isn't a real planet. They think Pluto used to be one of Neptune's moons, until, for some reason, it stopped traveling around Neptune. Now Pluto travels around the sun all by itself. It has one tiny moon named Charon. Together, Pluto and Charon make the long, long journey in the dark.

How many moons does Neptune have? So far, scientists have found only two. They are named Nereid and Triton.

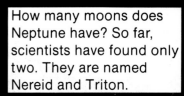

Triton

Nereid

27

SNOWBALLS AND SKY ROCKS

The Comet Story

The comet story begins in the farthest part of our solar system. Scientists think there is a great cloud billions of miles past Pluto. The cloud is in an icy-cold part of space. It is like a refrigerator…a comet refrigerator!

The frozen comets wait together in the cloud. They are waiting for a passing star to bump them out of the cloud. Sometimes a comet has to wait billions of years. But one day the lucky comet gets knocked out of the cloud, and it starts its long, long journey in toward the sun.

Comets are like ghosts in space. They are hardly made of anything at all. We can send a spacecraft to fly right by a comet, but we could never land on a comet. There is nothing to land on! A comet is just a big dirty snowball. It is made of dust, ice, and gases. Some of the gases are the same ones in the air we breathe, but some of them are poison.

Years pass. The comet speeds along on its journey. It is leaving the comet cloud far behind. After a great while, the comet reaches the orbit of Pluto. It shoots by Neptune. It whizzes past Uranus, and Saturn, and Jupiter. Every moment the comet is getting closer and closer to the sun.

Now the people on Earth can see the comet. The sun's light and heat are making the comet lose some of its dust and gas. The dust and gas stream out behind the comet. This is the comet's tail. It is millions of miles long, but it is so thin, you can see stars twinkling through it.

Sometimes the comet's tail splits into two parts. Sometimes it splits into three parts! Then the comet looks like it is waving glittering streamers behind it.

The comet flies on. It makes a sharp turn around the sun. Now the comet's tail is in the front. The comet passes Mercury, Venus, and Earth. It passes Mars. The comet is heading back to outer space.

Comets are real members of our solar system. They travel around the sun just like the planets, but some comets have very, very far to go. It can take them thousands of years to circle the sun once.

The most famous comet of all is Halley's Comet. It has been seen every 76 years since the year 240 BC! No wonder it is famous!

But comets do not live forever. Every time a comet passes the sun, the sun melts some of its ice. It blows away some of the gas. The comet gets smaller and smaller. At last the comet breaks apart, but it leaves behind all the broken bits and pieces of itself. The bits and pieces keep circling the sun just the way the comet did. Then, whenever the comet pieces get close to the sun, some of them fall to Earth in a sparkling shower.

Meteors and Meteorites

A meteor is a visitor from outer space. Some people call meteors shooting stars, but meteors are not stars. They are chunks of iron and stone. Scientists think most meteors are broken pieces of asteroids, so meteors are really space junk!

Meteors fall to Earth very, very fast. They are not at all like comets. You can see a comet in the night sky for many days, but don't blink, or you will miss a meteor.

As a meteor falls it starts to get hot. Soon it is glowing brightly. The meteor is burning up. Many meteors burn up completely before they reach Earth, but sometimes a meteor is big enough to last the whole trip. Closer and closer it comes. Faster and faster it races. The meteor can't slow down. It has to make a crash-landing! The meteor hits the ground so hard, it forms a deep crater. The meteor is much smaller than when it started, but it can still weigh thousands of tons. A meteor that makes it all the way to Earth is called a meteorite.

A few times a year midnight sky watchers get a real treat. A broken comet flies by Earth, and for about two days meteors, and meteors, and meteors fall from the sky! The meteors are pieces of the comet. If the night is very dark, you can see 50 or 60 in one hour. That's a meteor every minute. Scientists call this a meteor shower.

The Barringer Meteor Crater in Arizona is almost 600 feet deep. The meteorite that made this giant crater weighed more than a million pounds. When the meteorite hit, it crushed all the rocks on the ground under it. Many of the rocks melted from the terrible heat.

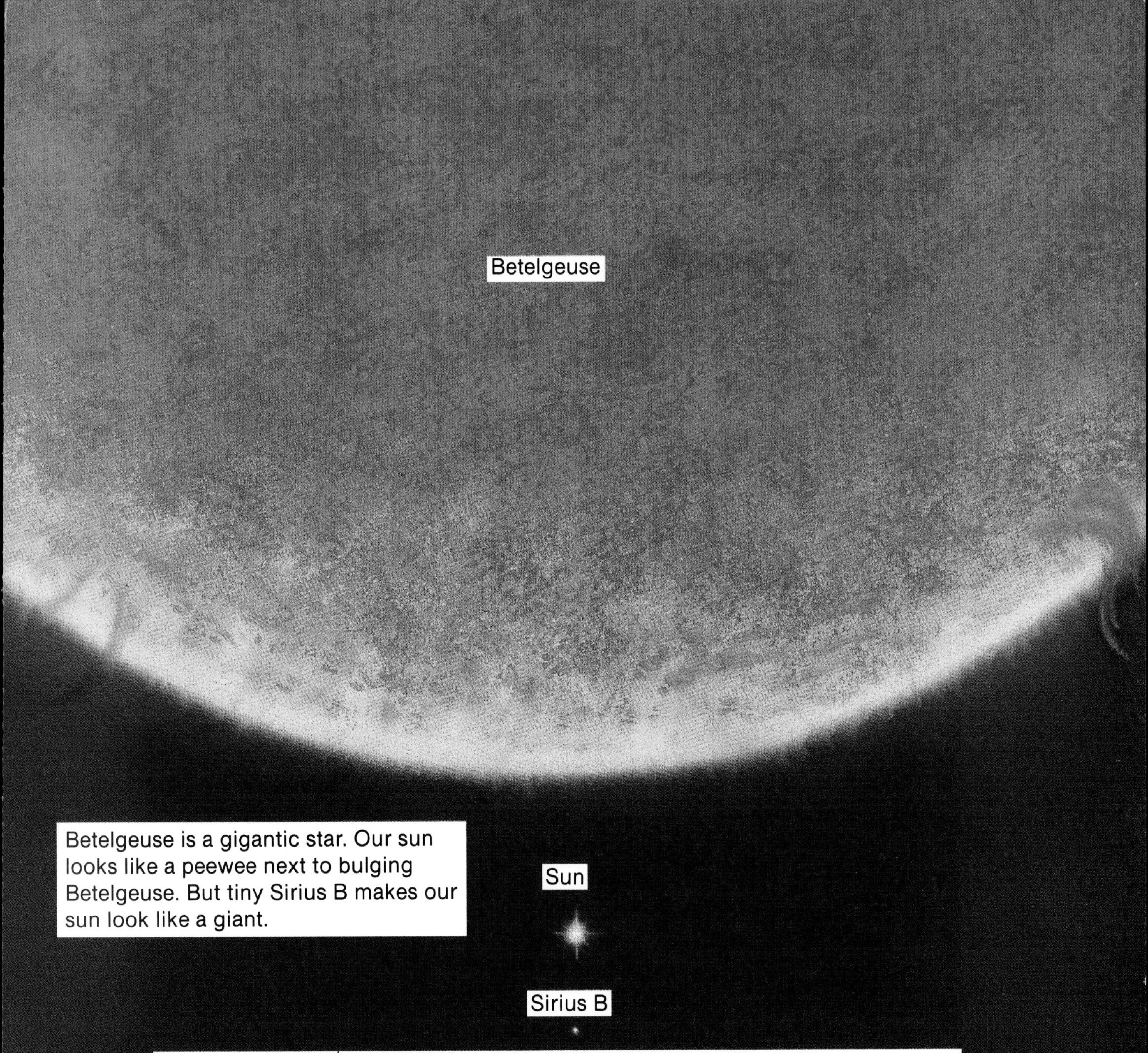

Betelgeuse

Betelgeuse is a gigantic star. Our sun looks like a peewee next to bulging Betelgeuse. But tiny Sirius B makes our sun look like a giant.

Sun

Sirius B

ONCE UPON A STARRY NIGHT

There are billions and billions of stars, but we can only see about 2,000 of them. That's because most stars are too far away. Even astronomers can't see all the stars through their great telescopes, but they know the stars are out there.

Stars look like little bits of silver in the night sky, but they are really great balls of hot gas. Some stars are just like our sun. They are not too big and not too small. They are just average. But stars can be stranger than strange. They can be mighty monsters. They can be smaller than Earth. There are even red stars, black stars, and invisible stars.

This is Trifid Nebula. Nebula means "cloud." The Trifid Nebula is a birth cloud. Baby stars are being born here.

This is the Crab Nebula. Do you think it looks like a crab? The Crab Nebula is the ghost of a star that blew up more than 900 years ago. Now the Crab Nebula is spreading out and out and out through space.

Birth and Death

Stars are born from gas and dust. It takes nature millions of years to make a star, but the time is not wasted. Stars last for billions of years. They light up the nighttime sky with their silver beauty. But stars cannot keep burning forever. So one day every star must stop shining. Every star must die.

As a small star gets older it begins to cool off. Its light grows dimmer and dimmer. Finally the star flickers and dies. Its light and heat slowly fade away. All that is left is a cold dark ball of ashes.

When a large star dies, it lights up the sky! First it puffs up like a balloon. It gets bigger and bigger. If there are any nearby planets, the dying star swallows them. Then, when the star can't get any bigger, it explodes. Scientists call these kinds of stars novas. When a really big star explodes, it is called a supernova.

These bright stars are called the Pleiades. How many do you count? There are about 3,000 stars here. The Pleiades are very young stars. They were born just a few million years ago.

This star is "stretching." A black hole is pulling at the star's gas like a vacuum cleaner sucking up dust. Someday the black hole may swallow the whole star.

The strangest star of all is one that nobody can see. It is called a black hole. Only the very biggest stars can become black holes when they die. These stars don't explode. First they puff up and up and up, growing in size until they are GIGANTIC! Then, instead of bursting apart, they squash. They pack themselves into a tight, tiny ball. They get smaller than anything we can ever imagine. They get smaller than a dot!

And then they disappear from sight.

But how do astronomers know that there are really black holes in space if they can't see them?

Black holes are like vacuum cleaners. Everything that gets close to a black hole falls into it. Black holes can swallow rockets, planets, and even other stars. And there is no way to escape. Black holes are traps. They are the scariest stars in the sky.

Astronomers are searching the sky with their telescopes. They are looking for funny-shaped stars. If a star looks like it is all stretched out, maybe it's because it is near a black hole. Maybe the "cosmic vacuum cleaner" is at work.

Why Everyone Doesn't See the Same Stars

Look up in the sky at night. What do you see? You see a sky shining bright with stars. But if you live in Canada or the United States, you don't see the same stars as someone who lives in Australia. Why?

Earth is a giant ball hanging in space. Space is filled with stars, so there are stars all around Earth. There are people all around Earth, too, so everyone who looks up into the sky can see hundreds of stars.

Here are two people standing on Earth. One person lives in Canada. The other person lives in Australia. The person from Canada looks up. He sees all kinds of stars. He sees the friendly stars of the Big Dipper. But now let's travel to Australia.

Welcome to Australia! The sky over Australia is filled with stars, too, but many of these stars do not look familiar at all. That's because we are looking at a different part of the sky. The stars in the Big Dipper are gone. They are in a part of the sky we can't see from Australia.

The Story of Polaris

If you live in the Northern Hemisphere, you can see Polaris in summer and winter. You can see it in spring and fall. Night after night, good old Polaris is in the very same place in the sky. Polaris never changes. Polaris is the pole star.

If you could draw a line from Earth's North Pole all the way up into the sky, you would reach Polaris. Polaris sits right over the North Pole, so Polaris was a very important star to the early sailors. It helped them sail the great oceans without losing their way.

Most stars rise in the east and set in the west, but not Polaris. Polaris stays put all year long and all night long. Polaris is in the center of a glittering star merry-go-round. About 50 bright stars circle Polaris. These stars do not rise and set either. They just go round and round Polaris, so they are called circumpolar stars. Circumpolar means "around the Pole."

If you are in the Northern Hemisphere, Polaris is high in the sky. But as you go farther and farther south, Polaris seems to move lower and lower in the sky. When you stand right at the equator, Polaris is so low, it is right on the horizon. When Polaris started to sink in the sky, the sailors knew they were traveling south. When Polaris rose in the sky, the sailors knew they were traveling north.

The Constellations

There are pictures in the sky. The pictures are made of stars, and they are called constellations, which means "with stars." There are 88 constellations in all. Some are pictures of fabulous animals from Greek stories. There are horses that fly and terrible monsters. There are brave heroes and glittering birds. The constellations are a little hard to find at first, but with a little practice, you will be able to see them shining high above you.

The most famous constellation of all is Ursa Major. Ursa Major means "the Great Bear." It takes many stars to form Ursa Major, but the seven stars that make up Ursa Major's body are very bright and easy to see. They look like a giant pot, so they are known as the Big Dipper.

Ursa Major turns round and round Polaris, so it is a circumpolar constellation. You can see it all year long, because most of Ursa Major never sets.

There are four other circumpolar constellations. They are Draco the Dragon, Cassiopeia the Queen, Cepheus the King, and Ursa Minor the Little Bear. But Ursa Minor looks like a pot, too, so it is nicknamed the Little Dipper. The last star in Ursa Minor's tail is Polaris.

To find Polaris, look high overhead on a clear dark night. Look for a huge square with a crooked handle. That's the Big Dipper. Find the two front stars in the Big Dipper's bowl. Follow them up. You will come to a bright star almost exactly over your head. That's Polaris. Polaris is also the last star in the Little Dipper's handle (which is also Ursa Minor's tail).

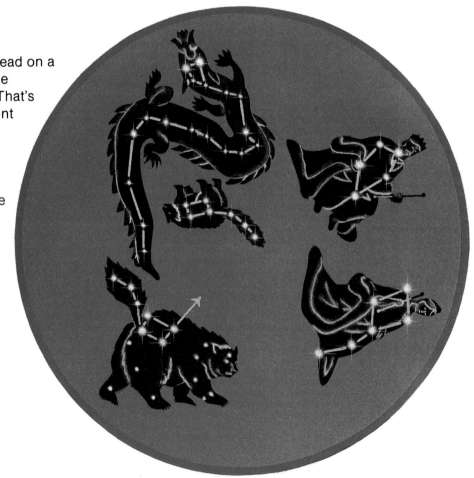

The Constellations of the Zodiac

The zodiac is a group of twelve constellations. The constellations of the zodiac are lined up one after the other, all around the sky. They are like charms on a bracelet. Every month a different zodiac constellation rises in the east. As the days pass, you can see more and more of it. After about 30 days, the whole constellation is above the horizon. But keep watching! In a year you will be able to see all twelve constellations.

Most of the constellations in the zodiac are animals, but there are people, too. Sagittarius is an archer that carries a gleaming bow and arrow. Sagittarius is a big and fairly bright constellation, but it doesn't really look too much like an archer. It looks more like a teapot!

Gemini the Twins is hard to see. Most of the stars are too dim and far away, but if you know just where to look, you can see the twins' heads. They are the stars Castor and Pollux.

Taurus the Bull is right next to Gemini. Taurus is dim, too, but it has a flaming red eye. Taurus' eye is the beautiful star Aldebaran. Aldebaran is so big, nearly 300 suns lined up one after the other would fit around the middle of Aldebaran.

Scorpius the Scorpion is one of the biggest constellations in the zodiac, and it really looks like a scorpion! You can easily see Scorpius' long tail and sharp claws.

The great galaxy in Andromeda

Galaxies

Our sun travels through space with billions of other stars. We are all part of a great star family called a galaxy. If you look into the sky on a summer night, you can see part of our galaxy. Look for a wide band of light stretching across the sky. The band of light comes from the stars at the edge of our galaxy.

The ancient people gave our galaxy a name. They called it the Milky Way. They thought the band of stars in our galaxy looked like spilled milk. Maybe the milk came from the Big Dipper!

Scientists have never seen the Milky Way from far out in space, but they are pretty sure that it is shaped like a giant pinwheel. The Milky Way even turns like a pinwheel. That's because all the stars in the Milky Way are moving around in the same direction. The sun moves around the Milky Way, too, but even though it moves fast, it still takes a very long time to make one turn. It takes the sun 220 million years to go once around the galaxy.

The Milky Way has some galaxy neighbors. One galaxy is called M31. It is also known as the great galaxy in Andromeda. M31 is shaped like a pinwheel, too. Even if you could travel as fast as a beam of light, it would take you more than two million years to get to M31.

This galaxy doesn't have a name. Scientists just call it NGC 5128. NGC 5128 is one of the strangest galaxies in the universe. It is not shaped at all like a normal galaxy. It is also sending out weird radio waves.

Astronomers can see thousands of galaxies through their great telescopes. Most of the galaxies are bunched together in groups. The Milky Way belongs to a group of 25 galaxies called the Local Group. Not too long ago astronomers discovered a new member of our group. The new galaxy is close to the Milky Way, so astronomers nicknamed it Snickers, after the candy bar. Now the Local Group has a Milky Way and a Snickers!

Astronomers can see something else through their telescopes. They can see that all the galaxies are flying away from each other. They are spreading out in all directions. What's happening?

Most scientists think that once upon a time, everything in the universe was jammed together. It was packed very, very, very tight in a tiny ball. Scientists call this ball the cosmic egg. The cosmic egg was hotter than anything can ever be. It was tinier than anything can ever be. It was the whole universe in a little hot dot!

All at once the cosmic egg exploded. Everything in the cosmic egg shot off in all directions. Scientists call this explosion the Big Bang, and they think it happened about 20 billion years ago. Today the galaxies are slowing down, but they are still moving away from each other. Will they ever stop? No one knows. It is one of the great mysteries of the universe.

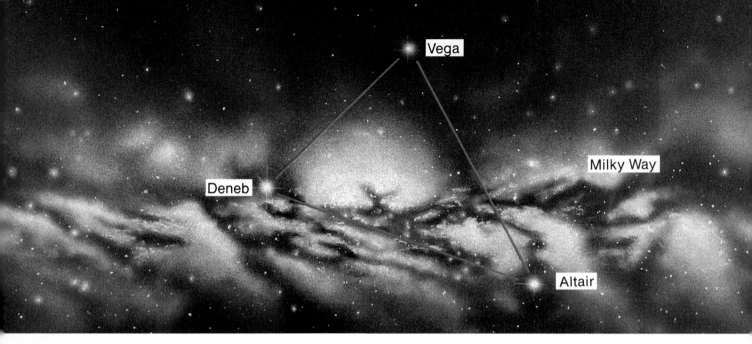

How to Find Vega

Think BIG! Look for a huge triangle high overhead in the summer sky. The triangle is made of three very bright stars. Two of the stars are right in the middle of the band of light we call the Milky Way. The third star is sitting on the right bank of the Milky Way. That's Vega.

HEY! IS ANYBODY OUT THERE?

Is our sun the only star that has planets? Most scientists say no. They think there are a lot of other planets in space, but planets are very hard to find. They are small and dark and do not shine brightly like stars, so scientists can't see them through their telescopes.

But…

Scientists think they have found something very exciting. They think they have found a huge solar system cloud. The cloud is made of gas and dust, and it is circling a star that is easy to see in the summertime. The star's name is Vega.

The cloud looks like a giant doughnut. Vega is right in the middle of the doughnut hole.

Scientists hope that the Vega cloud will begin to get lumpy. Then maybe the lumps will form planets. But the scientists will have to wait a long time to see anything. It takes many millions of years to make a solar system from scratch. It's a big job!

The Vega cloud is a promise that something wonderful may happen one day far into the future. It is the promise of a new solar system. So maybe, just maybe, we are not alone after all….

A few years ago an astronomer named Frank Drake tried an experiment. It was called Project Ozma. Many scientists worked on Project Ozma. Day after day they listened to noises coming from outer space. They used a special kind of telescope that could hear faint signals far, far away. Dr. Drake knew he would not be able to see people on other planets, but if they were sending messages, he thought, maybe we could hear them.

Dr. Drake and his team tried and tried, but they didn't hear a peep that sounded like a message. Then Dr. Drake thought of something.

"Hey!" he said. "Maybe nobody is sending messages. Maybe everyone is listening! Let's send a message!"

Dr. Drake's message looks a little bit like this:

DOT…DOT DOT DOT…DOT DOT…DOT DOT DOT DOT…DOT DOT

The dots are a code. When the code is broken, the message forms a picture that tells all about us. It is a big hello from Earth. Maybe someday creatures from another planet will hear our message and answer us. And that would be the greatest message of all.

Astronomers use giant bowl-shaped transmitters to send radio waves into space.

41

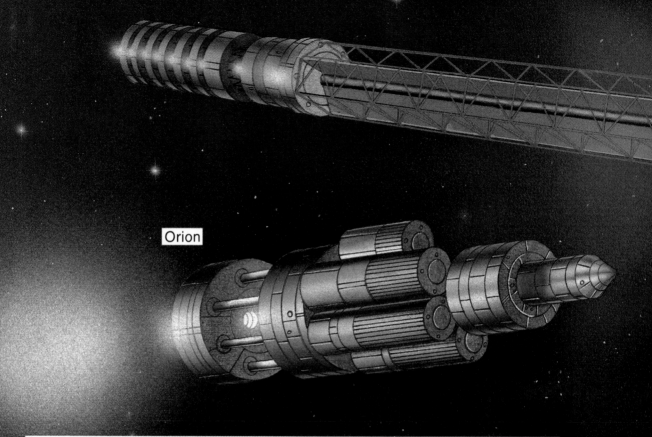

Orion

ROCKET WINGS AND SPEEDY THINGS

Scientists have big dreams. They want to speed through the solar system on rocket wings. They want to visit other planets and explore strange new worlds. They want to cross the galaxy. But the universe is a very big place. There are great wide-open spaces between the stars, so the best rocket we have would not be any good at all.

Our best rocket is called the *Saturn V*. The *Saturn V* helped *Apollo* get to the moon, but it could never get us to the stars. It's much too slow, and it doesn't even have room for passengers.

The *Saturn V* is called a booster rocket. Its job is to give smaller spacecraft a boost into space. So the *Saturn V* is nothing but gas tanks and engines. And they're not very fast engines, either. If we used the *Saturn V* for really long trips, we'd be sunk! A voyage to the nearest star would take a whole lifetime. A voyage across the Milky Way would take a million lifetimes!

So the scientists said, "Hey! Let's not use the *Saturn V*! Let's design a new ship. Let's design a better ship! A faster ship!"

Bussard Ramjet

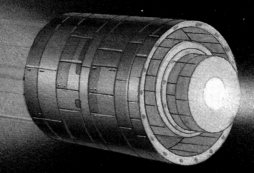

These rocket ships are in the planning stages. They are very complicated and hard to build, but scientists are pretty sure that someday soon they will be able to solve all the building problems. Then maybe these great ships will carry us across the galaxy to strange new worlds.

Many years ago the United States government planned to build a very fast spaceship named *Orion*. *Orion* would have been much faster than the *Saturn V* rocket. It would also have had room for some passengers. *Orion* could have traveled all the way to Pluto and back in three months, but *Orion* never got the chance to carry people to the stars. The scientists had other plans. They were coming up with better and better starship designs.

One of the designs for a fabulous new starship looks like it was drawn by aliens. It is called the *Bussard Ramjet*. It was named after the scientist who designed it, Dr. Robert Bussard. But Dr. Bussard is not an alien. He is just a very clever human being.

The *Bussard Ramjet* would be gigantic! It would shoot through space at very fast speeds, so it could carry us to distant planets easily. But there is one little problem. No one can figure out how to build it—not even Dr. Bussard.

But there is a ship that we can build right away. It is called the *Echolance*. It was designed by Dr. Robert Duncan-Enzmann in 1949. The *Echolance* would be so fast, it would take us across the galaxy in a few years, and there would be plenty of room inside for thousands of voyagers.

Someday, sooner than you think, the dream of space travel will come true. So pack your suitcase. The stars are waiting....

INDEX

A

Aldebaran, 37
Andromeda Galaxy (M31), 38
Apollo, 19, 42
Asteroids, 22, 30
Atmosphere
    on Earth, 17
    on Mercury, 14
    on the Moon, 18
    on Venus, 15

B

Barringer Meteor Crater, 30
Betelgeuse, 31
Big Bang, 39
Big Dipper, 36, 38. *See also*
    Ursa Major.
Black Holes, 33
Bussard Ramjet, 43

C

Cassiopeia, 36
Castor and Pollux, 37
Cave dwellers, 6
Cepheus, 36
Ceres, 22
Clavius Crater, 19
Comets, 28–29, 30
Constellations, 36–37.
    See also Zodiac.
Continents, 17
Corona, 13
Cosmic egg, 39
Crab Nebula, 32
Craters
    on asteroids, 22
    Barringer, 30
    on Callisto, 24
    on Mercury, 14
    meteor, 30
    on the moon, 19

D

Draco, 36
Drake, Frank, 41
Duncan-Enzmann, Robert, 43

E

Earth, 16–17, 18
    year on, 12–13
Echolance, 43
El Caracol, 8

G

Galaxies, 38–39
Galilean satellites, 9, 24
Galileo, 9, 24
Gemini, 37
Great Red Spot, 23
Greeks, 7

H

Halley's Comet, 29
Huygens, Christian, 25

J

Jupiter, 9, 23, 24

L

Little Dipper, 36. *See also*
    Ursa Minor.
Local Group, 39

M

Mars, 12, 20–21
Mercury, 14, 15, 24
Meteor crater. *See* Barringer
    Meteor Crater.
Meteorites, 30
Meteors, 16, 30
Meteor shower, 30
Mexicans, 8

Milky Way galaxy, 38, 39
Moon, the, 9, 13, 18–19
Moons. *See* Satellites.

N

Neptune, 27
NGC 5128 (galaxy), 39
Novas, 32

O

Observatories. *See* El Caracol.
Orbits of planets, 10
Orion rocket, 43

P

Planetoids. *See* Asteroids.
Planet rings
   Jupiter, 23
   Saturn, 9, 25
   Uranus, 26
Planets
   discovered by Greeks, 7
   outside the solar system, 40
   visible with naked eye, 9.
   See also planet names.
Pleiades, 32
Pluto, 12, 27
Polaris, 35, 36
Pole star. *See* Polaris.
Project Ozma, 41

R

Rings. *See* Planet rings.

S

Sagittarius, 37
Satellites
   Jupiter, 24
   Neptune, 27
   Pluto, 27
   Saturn, 25
   Uranus, 26. *See also*
     Galilean satellites.
  Saturn, 25

Saturn V, 42, 43
Scorpius, 37
Search for alien life, 40–41
Shooting stars. *See* Meteors.
Sirius B, 31
Snickers galaxy, 39
Solar eclipse, 13
Solar system, 10–11
Stars, 6–7, 31–39
   age, 32
   birth, 32
   circumpolar, 35
   death, 32
   and early farmers, 7
   in navigation, 7, 35
   shooting. *See* Meteors.
   size, 31
   visible with naked eye, 31
Sun, 12–13
Supernovas, 32

T

Taurus, 37
Telescopes
   first, 9
   to look at the sun, 12
Trifid Nebula, 32

U

Uranus, 26
Ursa Major, 36
Ursa Minor, 36

V

Vega, 40
Venus, 8, 15
Volcanoes
   on Europa, 24
   on Io, 24
   on Mars, 21
   on Mercury, 14
Voyager, 23, 24, 25, 26

Z

Zodiac, 37